A HISTORICAL ALBUM OF

FLORIDA

A HISTORICAL ALBUM OF

FLORIDA

Charles A. Wills

THE MILLBROOK PRESS, Brookfield, Connecticut

Front and back cover: "Sir Francis Drake Attacks St. Augustine," London, 1589. Courtesy of Hans and Hanni Kraus, Sir Francis Drake Collection, Rare Book Division, Library of Congress.

Title page: A pond in central Florida. Courtesy of the Florida Phosphate Council.

Library of Congress Cataloguing-in-Publication Data

Wills, Charles.
    A historical album of Florida / Charles A. Wills.
        p. cm. — (Historical albums)
    Includes bibliographical references and index.
    Summary: A history of Florida, from its early days to its rapid rise
in population and importance in the twentieth century.
    ISBN 1-56294-480-0 (lib. bdg.)   ISBN 1-56294-760-5 (pbk.)
    1. Florida—History—Juvenile literature. 2. Florida—
Gazetteers—Juvenile literature. [1. Florida—History] I. Title.
II. Series.
F311.3.W55 1994
975.9—dc20   93-35016
                                           CIP
                                           AC

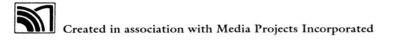 Created in association with **Media Projects Incorporated**

    C. Carter Smith, *Executive Editor*
    Lelia Wardwell, *Managing Editor*
    Charles A. Wills, *Principal Writer*
    Bernard Schleifer, *Art Director*
    Shelley Latham, *Production Editor*
    Arlene Goldberg, *Cartographer*

    Consultant: Alan Kay, Horace Mann Junior High School,
Palm Harbor, Florida

C O N T E N T S

Introduction

Few states can boast a history as long or as varied as Florida's. Thousands of years ago, Florida was the homeland of a flourishing Native American culture. The first European known to have visited Florida, Juan Ponce de León, arrived in 1513, just two decades after Christopher Columbus's first voyage to the New World. In 1565—more than a half-century before the Pilgrims landed in Massachusetts—Spanish colonists founded St. Augustine, the first permanent European settlement on land that would one day become the United States. Over the next three centuries, the flags of five nations—Spain, France, Great Britain, the United States, and the Confederate States of America—would fly over all or part of Florida.

But much of Florida's history is recent. Not long ago, Florida was a land of ranches, farms, and fishing villages, of vast swamps and endless pine forests. In the 19th and 20th centuries, wave after wave of newcomers—tourists, planters, railroad builders and real-estate developers, retirees and refugees—transformed Florida into the nation's fourth-largest state.

Despite its amazing growth, much of the old Florida remains, side-by-side with the new. Modern Florida is a state of palm trees and skyscrapers, spaceships and swamps, superhighways and slow-moving rivers. It is home to a diverse population, with citizens from every corner of the globe. Today, Florida is a state where both past and future come together.

FLORIDA UNDER MANY FLAGS

France and Spain were rivals for control of Florida in the 16th and 17th centuries. This engraving shows French explorer Jean Ribaut's ships off the Florida coast in 1562.

Florida's history began thousands of years ago, when Native Americans first arrived in the region. With Ponce de León's voyage in 1513, Spain became the first European nation to stake a claim to Florida. Except for two decades under British rule, Spain held onto Florida until the early 19th century, when the United States took control. After achieving statehood in 1845, Florida was the site of a long conflict between Native Americans of the Seminole nation and the U.S. Army. The Seminole Wars were barely over before the Civil War began. Florida joined the Confederacy, and it was not until 1868 that the state was re-admitted to the Union.

Florida's Early Inhabitants

About 20,000 years ago, people from Asia began to arrive in North America, landing in the region we now call Alaska. They crossed a bridge of land, now vanished, that connected the two continents. Over thousands of years, these Native Americans (mistakenly called "Indians" by European explorers) spread across North America. Between 10,000 and 15,000 years ago, groups of Native Americans reached the finger of land known today as Florida. These early Floridians moved from place to place, living by hunting and by gathering shellfish along the coasts of the Atlantic Ocean and the Gulf of Mexico.

Around 5000 BC, Florida's Native Americans began living in permanent villages. Over the following centuries, these early Floridians came to rely less on hunting and more on farming, growing crops of corn, beans, and squash. They made some of the earliest pottery in North America. They buried their dead in large mounds and later built temples atop the mounds. Florida's Native Americans also traded with other Native American groups throughout North America. Ancient shells from Florida have been found in present-day Illinois and Ohio.

By 1500 AD, about the time European explorers reached North and South America, there were between 10,000 and 25,000 people living in Florida. These people were divided into several groups, or tribes. The Calusas lived in southern Florida along the Atlantic Coast. The east, or Gulf Coast, was home to the Tegestas and Tumucuas. The Apalachee, Pensacola, and Chatot tribes lived in northwest Florida, in the region now called the Panhandle. In the Florida Keys, a chain of islands reaching south into the Caribbean Sea, lived the Arawaks and the Matecumbes. Of all of these tribes, the Calusas were the most powerful. A fierce, warlike people, the Calusas had control over most of southern Florida. European ships were a source of wealth for the Calusas, who collected cargo that washed ashore from shipwrecks.

Within 250 years of the European discovery of Florida, almost all the region's Native Americans were gone. A handful escaped to other parts of North America when Spanish explorers began their conquest of Florida in the 1500s. Others were sold into slavery in Spain's Caribbean colonies. Many died of unfamiliar diseases brought by the Europeans, or were killed in battle with the newcomers. Even the warlike Calusas were no match for the swords, guns, and attack dogs of the Spanish *conquistadors* (conquerors).

For some of Florida's Native Americans, war was a way of life. This engraving (right), based on the work of Jacques Le Moyne, shows a Florida warrior armed with a bow and poison-tipped arrows.

Because of Florida's warm climate, Native American shelters were usually simple structures. This 19th-century engraving (below) depicts a common type of dwelling—a grass-roofed, wood-framed hut with a raised platform for sleeping.

In Search of the Fountain of Youth

No one is sure when the first Europeans sighted Florida or set foot on its shores. Spanish sea captains, who took the lead in exploring what Europeans called the "New World," may have seen the Florida coast as early as 1497 —just five years after Christopher Columbus's first voyage. The Florida peninsula appears on a map drawn by a Portuguese explorer in 1502, but little is known about his expedition to the New World.

The first explorer known to have landed in Florida was Juan Ponce de León of Spain. De León, a soldier from a noble family, was an experienced explorer, well known for his conquest of the Caribbean island of Puerto Rico in 1508. According to a popular story, de León heard Native Americans tell stories of a wonderful land called Bimini, where a spring flowed with magical water that made people young forever. It is now believed that this story of the "Fountain of Youth" was probably made up by later writers. When de León sailed for Florida in 1512, he was not seeking a fountain of youth, but more land and gold for Spain, and converts for the Roman Catholic Church.

In April 1513, de León's three ships reached Florida. It was Ponce de León who gave Florida its name. According to some accounts, de León chose the name "Florida" because the expedition arrived at Easter, which is called *Pascua Florida* (the Feast of Flowers) in Spanish. Other historians believe de León was inspired by the region's lush landscape, because the word "Florida" means "full of flowers" in Spanish.

De León found no gold or other riches, and after clashing with the local Native Americans, the expedition returned to Cuba. Eight years later, de León returned to Florida. This time he hoped to establish a Spanish colony near Tampa Bay. The venture failed when a Native American's arrow hit de León, who soon died of his wound.

For the next four decades, Spain tried to colonize Florida, with little

Explorers marveled at Florida's swamps and the many kinds of wildlife they contained. This 19th-century engraving (opposite, top) shows the variety of species to be found in the wetlands—flamingos, cranes, egrets, turtles, and the often dangerous alligator.

Born in San Servos, Spain, Juan Ponce de León (opposite, bottom) arrived in what Europeans called the "New World" in 1493 as a member of Christopher Columbus's second expedition. Before he set out from Cuba in 1513, Spanish officials appointed him governor of any new lands he might discover.

Published in Germany in 1591, this map (below) is an early—and not very accurate—view of Florida. The Spanish colony at St. Augustine was already twenty-six years old when the map was drawn.

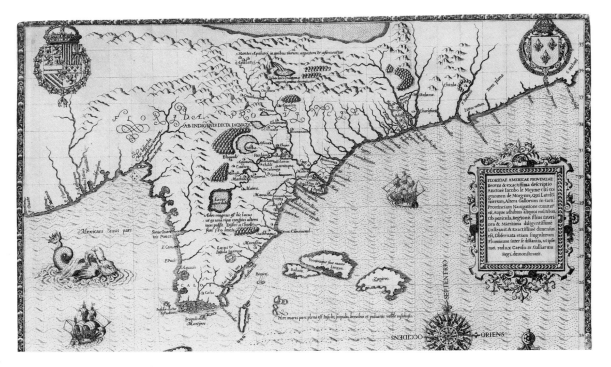

success. In 1528, an expedition led by Pánfilo de Narváez met a series of disasters that led to the deaths of all but four of the expedition's 242 men. In 1539, Hernando de Soto explored a lot of Florida, but failed to establish any lasting settlements. The most ambitious attempt to build a colony came in 1559, when Tristán de Luna led 1,500 settlers from Mexico to what is now Pensacola. A hurricane destroyed the struggling colony the following year, forcing the survivors to return to Mexico.

France soon became interested in Florida. In 1562, French explorer Jean Ribaut reached the mouth of the St. Johns River, near what is now Jacksonville. Two years later, another Frenchman, René de Laudonnière, led a group of French settlers to the banks of the St. Johns. They built a settlement named Fort Caroline in honor of the queen of France.

King Philip II of Spain believed that the French were trespassing on Spanish territory. The settlers at Fort Caroline were Huguenots (French Protestants), and this angered the Catholic monarch. In 1565, Spanish forces attacked Fort Caroline and killed almost all of the French settlers.

The Struggle for Florida

On a site near the ruins of Fort Caroline, the Spanish built a settlement named St. Augustine. Under the firm leadership of Pedro Menéndez de Avilés, St. Augustine became the first permanent European settlement in what would become the United States.

St. Augustine barely survived in its early years. Because of its location on the coast, the settlement was difficult to defend against attack. In 1586, the English sea captain Sir Francis Drake raided St. Augustine and burned it to the ground.

The building of the Castillo de San Marcos, near St. Augustine, shown in this 18th-century view, was a huge project. To provide labor, the Spanish relied on Indian and African slaves. The fort was completed in 1687.

While St. Augustine was being rebuilt, Spanish missionaries arrived, eager to convert Florida's surviving Native Americans to Catholicism. Eventually, a network of thirty-six missions (religious settlements) stretched across northern Florida. Thousands of Native Americans accepted Catholicism and came to live in the missions, where priests of the Franciscan religious order taught them European arts and crafts. A 17th-century bishop wrote that the

Native Americans were "clever and quick to learn any art they see done, and great carpenters." Spanish settlers also began raising cattle in the grasslands of central Florida, beginning a ranching industry that still exists today. But St. Augustine remained Spain's chief outpost in Florida.

Over the decades, St. Augustine grew into a large town, with houses, shops, and *tabernas* (taverns) built around a Spanish-style plaza. The townspeople included *peninsulares* (Spanish-born colonists), *criollos* (people of Spanish ancestry who were born in Florida), and African slaves. In addition, there were several Native American villages outside the town gates. Later, a settlement of free African Americans grew up near the town—one of the first such communities in North America.

In the 17th century, Spanish colonies in Florida became caught in the European struggle for control of North America. France was settling Canada and exploring the Mississippi River Valley, while England had started a string of colonies on the Atlantic Coast. Both England and France considered Spain their enemy. Since Florida was a partly settled region, it was a tempting target.

To counter the threat from France, Spanish authorities built a fort at Pensacola in western Florida in 1699. Twenty years later French forces would capture Pensacola, but the French eventually lost interest in Florida, and Spain regained control.

The greatest danger of attack came from the English colonies to the north. In 1672, work began on a massive fort to protect St. Augustine. Known as Castillo de San Marcos (the Castle of St. Mark), the fort was built of *coquina*, a local material made of tiny shells joined with lime. The fort was finally finished in 1687.

Seven years later, an expedition led by Governor James Moore of Carolina attacked St. Augustine. The invaders burned down the town, but most of the townspeople stayed safe inside the castillo's walls. Spanish warships soon arrived from Cuba and drove off Moore's forces.

The fort's walls and Spanish ships couldn't protect the missions in Florida's interior. In 1704, Moore again raided Florida with a force of British colonists and Native Americans from Georgia's Yamassee tribe. The raiders burned many missions, killing and dispersing the Native Americans and Franciscan priests. Later raids destroyed what few missions remained.

In 1740, and again in 1742, British colonial forces attacked St. Augustine. Both attempts failed.

It was not long, however, before Britain won Florida without firing a shot. The story began in 1754, when Britain and France went to war over control of Canada. The conflict, known in Europe as the Seven Years War and in America as the French and Indian War, spread throughout the world as other nations joined in. In 1761,

Spain decided to enter the war on France's side against the British.

The decision to side with France was an unfortunate mistake for Spanish Floridians. British forces soon captured Havana in Cuba. When the war ended in 1763, Spain was forced to give Florida to Britain in return for Havana, which was a vital port for Spain's overseas trade.

The British government divided Florida into two separate colonies—West Florida, with its capital at Pensacola, and East Florida, governed from St. Augustine. Settlers from Britain and other nations came to Florida, attracted by generous land grants. Large plantations, worked by African slaves, sprang up. Other settlers cut timber or raised oranges for export.

British rule in Florida was short-lived. In 1775, the thirteen British colonies north of Florida began a revolutionary war—"Tories" siding with Britain, and "Patriots" fighting for independence. Both West and East Florida, however, remained loyal to Britain. For this reason, more than 10,000 Tories relocated to Florida.

In 1777, France joined the war on the Patriots' side, against England. Spain followed France two years later. By 1781, Spanish forces led by Bernardo de Gálvez had captured West Florida. In 1783, the war ended in a Patriot victory—the thirteen English colonies became the United States. The peace treaty handed all of Florida back to Spain.

English naturalist and artist Mark Catesby traveled through Florida in the early 18th century. His book, *Natural History of Carolina, Florida, and the Bahama Islands*, published in 1731, includes drawings of many species of Florida wildlife, including this flamingo.

The American Era Begins

Once again, the Spanish flag flew over Florida. But how long could Spain hold onto its colony? Spain had always found it hard to govern Florida, and in the years ahead things would only get worse.

In the 1780s and 1790s, Florida's population included traders and settlers from Britain and the new United States, free blacks who had escaped from slavery in the Southern states, and two large Native American groups: the Creeks and the Seminoles. Most of the population in Florida at that time lived in the northern part of the peninsula.

The Creek Indians originally lived in Georgia, but they had been forced from their homelands by white settlement. Thousands migrated to Florida in the early 1700s. Some of the Creek villages in Florida stayed in communication with the Creeks that remained in Georgia. Others, called Seminoles from a Creek word meaning "the separate ones," set up their own communities. Unlike the Creeks, the Seminoles permitted escaped slaves to live in their villages.

Each group of Floridians had a different aim. The American settlers hoped that Florida would become part of the United States—a desire shared by many colonists. The Creeks, Seminoles, and ex-slaves wanted to be left alone. British citizens who lived in Florida were concerned mostly with trade. Thus, Spain had to deal with a restless, divided population.

In 1803, the United States bought the vast Louisiana Territory from France. Over the next decade, the U.S. government took control of West Florida up to the Pearl River. (Until this time, West Florida included a strip of the Gulf Coast that is now divided between Louisiana, Mississippi, and Alabama.) These events left Florida isolated—a Spanish-ruled area surrounded by American territory. Spain, weakened by European wars, knew it wouldn't be long before the United States moved to seize Florida. In 1812, American settlers in East Florida tried to speed things up by rebelling against Spain, but the revolt fell apart.

In that same year, the War of 1812 broke out between Britain and the United States. Despite Florida's status as a Spanish colony, British forces captured Pensacola to use as a naval base. General Andrew Jackson, a tough soldier-politician, led American forces into Florida, fighting British troops and Native Americans. He drove the British out of Pensacola in November of 1814. The Spanish governor was left with a ravaged city, many of its forts destroyed.

Many English and American traders and adventurers arrived in northern Florida in the years following the Revolutionary War. Among them was William Bowles, a Maryland-born Tory. This painting (above) shows Bowles with some Creek Indians. Bowles lived among the Creeks and was arrested in 1803 and sent to prison for plotting against Spanish officials.

This lithograph (right) shows General Andrew Jackson—known as "Old Hickory" to his soldiers and "Sharp Arrow" to his Native American enemies—on horseback.

Indians in Florida continued to travel north and raid the United States after the war's end. In 1818, acting without orders, General Jackson again invaded Florida. This was a serious matter, because the United States and Spain were at peace. But fortunately for Jackson, the U.S. government supported his actions.

In 1819, Spain bowed to American pressure. Adams and Spanish diplomat Luis de Onís signed a treaty granting Florida to the United States. In return, the United States agreed to pay $5 million to American settlers with legal claims against Spain. Political turmoil in Spain held up approval of the Adams-Onís treaty for two years. During that time, Jackson acted as military governor of the region.

In this engraving, Jackson's troops arrive at Pensacola on May 22, 1818, after a 300-mile march from Saint Marks. Two days later, the Spanish surrendered the settlement. Jackson had seized Pensacola once before, during the War of 1812.

The Long Fight of the Seminoles

On February 22, 1821, the Adams-Onís treaty went into effect. Florida was now officially part of the United States. In the spring of 1822, Congress organized the Territory of Florida and appointed Virginia-born William Duval as its first governor. The first meeting of the territorial government took place in Pensacola in July. Because the new territory lacked decent roads, it took officials from eastern Florida eight weeks to travel to Pensacola. Officials from western Florida had an even worse experience traveling to a meeting in St. Augustine the following year: They were shipwrecked while sailing around the coast, and one legislator drowned. Thus, the government decided to establish a territorial capital midway between the two towns. Tallahassee, a former Creek settlement, was chosen. The legislature first met there in March 1824 in a log cabin, which was soon replaced by a stone building.

The transportation situation quickly improved. By the end of 1826, a road connected Tallahassee with Pensacola and St. Augustine. Soon, steamboats began to appear on Florida's many rivers, opening the central part of the territory to settlement.

Although many new towns sprang up in "Middle Florida," a major obstacle stood in the way of settlement: the Seminoles. More than 5,000 Seminoles lived in Florida, on land that the newcomers wanted for their own.

The Seminoles proved willing to fight for their land, thanks mainly to the leadership of Osceola, son of a Creek mother and an English father. The trouble began in 1830, when the U.S. government began a policy of "removal" for Native Americans in

With only about 1,000 followers, Osceola kept 10,000 troops tied up in Florida. An army officer sketched this portrait of Osceola during peace talks in May 1837—six months before the Seminole leader was captured by trickery.

the South, including Florida. Under the removal policy, Native Americans had to leave their homelands to settle in an Indian Territory west of the Mississippi River. Most of the Creeks and some Seminoles accepted removal. Others refused to give up their land. Under Osceola and other leaders, the remaining Seminoles waged a long and bitter struggle for their homeland.

On December 28, 1835, a party of Seminoles attacked two companies of soldiers commanded by Major Francis Dade. Only three soldiers survived. The attack marked the start of the Second Seminole War. (Historians consider Andrew Jackson's invasion of 1817 the first.)

The Seminoles were masters of guerrilla warfare. Seminole war parties seemed to appear out of nowhere to attack forts and patrols, only to melt back into Florida's swamps and pine forests. Besides the Seminoles, U.S. troops had another deadly enemy: disease. Of the 1,500 or so soldiers who died in the Second Seminole War, only 22 percent died in battle. The rest fell to malaria and yellow fever.

In 1837, American general Thomas Jesup invited Osceola to a peace conference. Over Jesup's camp waved a white flag, the sign of a truce. When Osceola arrived, Jesup betrayed his trust by taking him prisoner—an act which angered many Americans. Sent to prison in South Carolina, the great Seminole leader died a few months later.

This engraving shows the largest battle of the Seminole wars, which took place on December 25, 1837, near the northeastern shore of Lake Okeechobee. A force of 1,000 U.S. troops and volunteers commanded by Colonel Zachary Taylor, a future U.S. president, defeated about 500 Seminoles led by Coacoochee, the major Seminole leader after Osceola's capture.

The U.S. Army used trained dogs, imported from Cuba, to hunt down Seminoles. In this lithograph the Seminoles defend themselves against men and dogs. The long, costly, and brutal war against the Seminoles was unpopular with many Americans.

If the army believed the capture of Osceola would end Seminole resistance, they were wrong. Fighting continued until 1842. But, eventually, the army wore down the Seminoles. By the end of 1843, almost 4,000 Seminoles had been removed to Indian Territory. "I have been hunted like a wolf," said one Seminole leader, "and now I am sent away like a dog."

A few Seminoles remained in Florida, and in 1855 the Third Seminole War broke out. It ended three years later with the army driving the surviving Seminoles into the Everglades in southern Florida. Their descendants live there today. Since the Seminoles never signed a peace treaty, they consider themselves still at war with the United States.

Statehood and Secession

Settlers continued to arrive in Florida, even during the Seminole Wars. Many of the newcomers in the 1830s were poor people from the upper South, attracted by low land prices. By the end of the decade, Florida's population was almost 50,000. Soon the territory would have enough people to qualify for admission to the Union as a state. In 1839, delegates who attended a territorial convention drafted a state constitution and asked the federal government for statehood.

It would be six years, however, before Florida achieved that goal. The problem was slavery. By this time, the nation's Northern states had outlawed slavery. In the Southern states, however, slavery was legal and vital to the region's economy. Almost half the territory's population were slaves. Florida sought admission as a slave state.

At this point in history, most people in the Northern states were not

This illustration from a book published in France shows how Florida's capitol building in Tallahassee looked in the early 1840s. After Florida became a state, Tallahassee also became an important business center; planters from Alabama and Georgia, as well as "Middle Florida," brought their cotton to Tallahassee to be sold and shipped north.

opposed to slavery in the South. Many Northerners, however, didn't want to see slavery spread into any new territories the nation might gain in the years ahead—a real possibility if Southern politicians controlled the national government. Southerners, on the other hand, feared that Northern politicians would outlaw slavery if they were in the majority. Thus, the federal government tried to admit new states in pairs—one free (non-slave) state, one slave state. This kept the political power of the North and South balanced, at least in the Senate.

In 1844, the Iowa Territory applied for admission as a free state. This cleared the way for Florida's admission as a slave state. On March 3, 1845, President John Tyler signed Florida's statehood bill into law, and the territory became the twenty-seventh state of the Union. William D. Mosely, a planter, was elected governor. David Levy Yulee and James Westcott, Jr., became the new state's first senators. (Yulee was also the first Jewish U.S. senator.)

Florida's population doubled in its first fifteen years of statehood—from 70,000 to 140,000. Railroads spurred the new state's growth by easing the transportation of goods and people. The first tracks, built in 1845, ran from Tallahassee to St. Mark's on the Gulf of Mexico. Other lines soon carried Florida products—mainly cotton, timber, and cattle—to the rest of the country.

But tragedy lay ahead for Florida, and for the entire nation. In the 1850s, the conflict between North and South over slavery grew increasingly bitter. In 1860, Abraham Lincoln, who was against the spread of slavery, won the presidential election. Unwilling to accept Lincoln's victory, the Southern states began to secede (withdraw) from the Union.

Richard Keith Call, a former territorial governor and one of Florida's most respected citizens, announced that secession "opened the gates of Hell." Few white Floridians shared his view. Support for secession was strong throughout the state. On January 10, 1861, a statewide convention voted for secession. In February, Florida joined with other Southern states to establish the Confederate States of America. Yet another Flag—the "stars and bars" of the Confederacy—would fly over Florida.

Eighteen sugarcane plantations were operating in 1845, the year Florida was admitted to the Union. Harvesting the cane—a job done by slaves—was hot, backbreaking, and often dangerous work (top, right).

Slaves on Florida's sugar and cotton plantations usually lived in crude, crowded cabins like the ones shown in this illustration (right).

Florida and the Civil War

In April 1861, Confederate forces shelled Fort Sumter—held by Northern troops in the harbor of Charleston, South Carolina—into surrender. The conflict between the Union and the Confederacy was now a civil war. The conflict would last four long years.

Only one major Civil War battle was fought on Florida soil, but the state played an important role in the Confederacy's war effort. More than 15,000 Floridians fought for the Confederacy. About one-third of these men lost their lives. (In addition, about 1,000 white Floridians and an equal number of Florida's free African Americans and escaped slaves served in the Union Army.) General Edmund Kirby Smith, a native Floridian, was one of the South's top officers. Stephen Mallory of Key West served as Secretary of the Navy in the Confederate Cabinet.

The state of Florida provided the Confederacy with supplies as well as soldiers and leaders. As much of the South came under Union control, beef from Florida's cattle ranches became an important part of the Confederate Army's diet. In those days, the only way to preserve meat was with salt, which Florida could make by boiling seawater. Florida also produced lumber, sugar, fish, and pork for the Confederacy.

Wearing uniforms of homespun cloth, Confederate recruits in northern Florida pose for this 1861 photograph. Historians believe that almost all white Floridian men of military age served in the Confederate forces at one time or another during the four years of the Civil War.

The women of Florida also made great contributions to the Confederate cause. With so many men away fighting in the Confederate Army, women ran the ranches, plantations, and businesses. Others prepared bandages and medicine, or served as nurses with the Southern forces.

Control of the waters around Florida was a key part of the Union's war plans. The Union hoped to strangle the South with a naval blockade. Union warships would seal off the South's seaports, keeping supplies from overseas from reaching the Confederacy.

To make the blockade work, the Union Navy needed bases for its ships, so Union forces moved quickly to capture ports on Florida's long coastline and offshore islands. Fort Pickens, which guarded the important gulf port of Pensacola, stayed in Union hands after the war broke out. Union forces also seized Fort Jefferson on the Dry Tortugas islands and Fort Taylor on Key West. As the war went on, many of Florida's coastal and riverside towns fell to the Union, including Tampa, Apalachicola, Jacksonville, and St. Augustine, where Union troops occupied the old Castillo de San Marcos.

With the Confederate Army busy fighting elsewhere in the South, the government could not spare soldiers to protect Florida's ports. But when Union troops threatened northern Florida, the center of the state's cattle industry, the Confederacy had to act.

In February 1864, 5,000 Union soldiers marched out of Jacksonville. They hoped to seize cattle and other supplies intended for the Confederate Army, and to capture the capital at Tallahassee. Rushing an equal number of Confederate troops to the area, Confederate general Joseph Finegan met the Union force at Olustee. The battle raged from noon to nightfall and ended with the Union troops in retreat back to Jacksonville. More than 2,500 soldiers were killed, wounded, or missing, most of them from the Union forces. Only the gallant stand of two black regiments kept the Union troops from being wiped out completely. Less than a year later, however, the Confederacy was on the edge of defeat. On April 1, Florida governor John Milton committed suicide. Two weeks later, the main part of the Confederate Army surrendered in Virginia. On May 20, Union troops finally marched into Tallahassee—the last Confederate capital east of the Mississippi River—to capture and haul down the Stars and Bars, the flag of the Confederacy.

In the first months of the war, fighting in Florida centered on Pensacola, site of an important shipyard and naval base. This engraving (opposite) shows how Pensacola appeared about the time the war broke out between North and South.

Florida and Alabama troops failed to capture Fort Pickens (shown above), an outpost on Santa Rosa Island, which guarded the entrance to Pensacola Bay.

THE SUNSHINE STATE

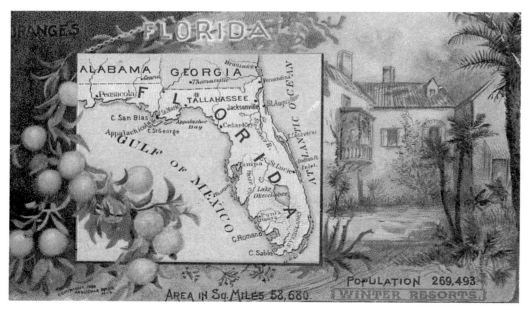

As this 1899 postcard shows, tourism and oranges were two of the keys to Florida's great growth in the last decades of the 19th century. Railroad builders and real estate promoters used posters, postcards, and pamphlets to advertise the state's charms.

The history of Florida from the end of the Civil War to the present day is a story of amazing growth. Beginning in the 1880s, tourism, railroads, citrus fruits, and other industries helped Florida prosper. Growth slowed after the famous real estate boom of the 1920s went bust, but after World War II, waves of newcomers—tourists, retirees, refugees from Cuba and other nations—made Florida one of the nation's fastest-growing states. Today, Florida tries to cope with the problems of growth, including damage to the state's fragile environment and the social problems caused by the flood of new residents.

Reconstruction and Revival

The war ended slavery in 1865, but African Americans in Florida and other Southern states were hardly better off. Thousands of Florida's newly freed slaves were homeless and hungry, and many faced violence at the hands of bitter, defeated whites. In addition, Florida's first postwar state government passed a series of harsh laws called "black codes." The laws kept African-American Floridians from voting, traveling freely, or enjoying other civil rights.

During the years after the war—a period known as Reconstruction—the federal government passed laws to safeguard the rights of African Americans, such as the Civil Rights Act of 1866. The states of the former Confederacy couldn't rejoin the Union until their governments agreed to respect these laws. Florida was forced to drop its black codes and adopt a more liberal state constitution. On July 25, 1868, Florida again took its place among the states of the Union.

Jacksonville became known as the Gateway to Florida during the passenger railroad boom of the late 19th century, when it went through tremendous growth. This bird's-eye view shows the city in 1893.

Orange Grove
St Johns River Flo.

Pruning

Scraping

Syringing

The new state constitution was a short-lived victory for Florida's black citizens. In the mid-1870s, the federal government lost interest in enforcing Reconstruction laws. Many white state governments quickly passed laws restricting the rights of African Americans. Segregation—forced separation of blacks and whites in education, public transportation, and restaurants—became a way of life in Florida for generations.

Despite the bitterness and conflict of Reconstruction, Florida made a fast recovery from the Civil War. The state still had few people and plenty of cheap land, so thousands of refugees from the war-ravaged South poured in. By 1880, the state's population reached almost 270,000.

Some people began to look at Florida as an up-and-coming state where great fortunes could be made. Three Northerners—Hamilton Disston, Henry Plant, and Henry Flagler—and two Southerners—William Chipley and Julia Tuttle—did the most to influence the growth of Florida in the last decades of the 19th century.

Chipley helped link the Panhandle to the rest of the state by building the Jacksonville, Pensacola, and Mobile Railroad, completed in 1882. Henry Plant did the same for the state's Gulf Coast. By constructing a network of railroads, warehouses, and shipping facilities, he turned Tampa from a small town into a major port. Disston bought 4 million acres of swampland from the state government. He drained and improved much of this land, opening up the South Florida wilderness to settlement.

Henry Flagler made his mark by developing Florida's tourism and citrus fruit industries. Thanks to its sunny weather, the state was already a popular destination for vacationers by the 1880s. Flagler bought land along the Atlantic Coast and built luxurious resort hotels to attract even more visitors. To bring people to the resorts, Flagler began work on the Florida East Coast Railway. By 1894, the railroad ran as far south as West Palm Beach. Flagler made plans to extend the line even farther south to Miami,

An 1875 newspaper illustration (opposite) shows several stages of orange cultivation. Twenty years later, a major frost forced Florida's growing citrus industry to move into the southern part of the state.

Phosphates—chemicals widely used to make fertilizer—boosted Florida's economy in the late 1800s. In 1883, deposits of phosphate-rich rock were found near Tampa, and phosphate mining quickly became an important industry. This photograph (top, right) shows phosphate prospectors digging near Dunellon in 1890.

Henry Flagler (right) made a fortune in the oil business before turning his talents and energy to developing resorts and railroads in Florida.

which at that time was no more than a tiny village.

Although the Spanish brought the first oranges to Florida, citrus fruits didn't become an important crop until the 19th century. But raising oranges and other citrus fruits was risky: A single bad frost could wipe out an entire harvest. The winter of 1894–95 was unusually cold for Florida. Much of the state's citrus industry was destroyed. Some citrus growers considered moving to South Florida, but many believed oranges wouldn't do well in the area's semi-tropical hot climate.

During that cold winter, Julia Tuttle, a Miami landowner and businesswoman, sent Henry Flagler a bundle of fresh orange blossoms—proof that citrus fruits could thrive in the region around Miami. Within a few years, groves of oranges, grape-fruits, lemons, and other fruits dotted the South Florida landscape. Because of her great salesmanship in this instance, Tuttle became known as the "Mother of Miami." Flagler's East Coast Railroad reached Miami in 1896, bringing tourists in and carrying fruit north to market. Miami soon became the state's leading resort city.

A steamboat brings visitors to Silver Springs in this 1886 photograph. Many Northerners came to Florida hoping that the warm, sunny climate would cure them of diseases like tuberculosis. According to a story popular at the time, a native Floridian told a visitor, "We live on sweet potatoes and sick Yankees."

Resorts and Resources

Promoters proclaimed Florida "America's playground," but tourists were not the only people coming to the state in the last years of the 19th century. Florida also attracted immigrants from around the country, and around the world.

In the early 1900s, people from the Greek islands began to settle at Tarpon Springs on the Gulf Coast north of Tampa. Many of these immigrants were sponge-divers—fishermen who dived to great depths to harvest sponges from the seabed. Sponge-diving declined after artificial sponges were developed, but Tarpon Springs remains home to a thriving Greek-American community.

People from Cuba and Spain also found new homes in Florida. Cuba was still a Spanish colony in the 19th century, and in 1868 a rebellion against Spanish rule broke out. Many

This 19th century advertisement for a sponge company shows some of the stages of gathering sponges and preparing them for market. In the main picture, men dive from boats to collect sponges from a reef bed. The sponges were dried, bleached, and trimmed before being sent to stores around the country.

of Cuba's cigar makers fled the fighting. Some went to Key West, others to New York. In the 1880s, one of the leading cigar manufacturers, Vicinte Martinez Ybor, decided to move his business to Tampa. Other cigar makers followed, and immigrants from Cuba and Spain soon arrived to provide labor. Eventually, there were 122 cigar factories in and around Tampa, producing 250 million cigars a year.

Rebellion again flared in Cuba in 1895. The Spanish government responded with brutal measures against the rebels and the island's civilian population. Most Americans sympathized with the Cubans in their fight for freedom, and some Floridians worked to aid the rebels. Adventurers, called "Filibusters," smuggled guns and ammunition into Cuba from Florida. One of the leading Filibusters was Napoleon Bonaparte Broward.

In April 1898, the United States and Spain went to war over Cuba. Thousands of U.S. troops left for the fighting in Cuba from the ports of Tampa and Jacksonville. The Spanish American War, which lasted only a few weeks, ended with Spain agreeing to give independence to Cuba.

Florida entered the 20th century with a population of 528,000—up from just over 300,000 in 1890. The year 1900 also saw Napoleon Broward's election as governor. Under Broward's leadership, the state drained much of the Everglades,

The grandest Florida resort was the Tampa Bay Hotel. Built by Henry Plant in 1901, the hotel, which is a quarter-mile long, set the standard for elegance. Today it is part of the campus of the University of Tampa.

opening even more of southern Florida to farming and settlement.

An unfortunate disaster hit northern Florida on May 1, 1901, when a fire swept through Jacksonville, leveling nearly 500 acres of the city. But Jacksonville made a quick recovery and soon surpassed Key West and Pensacola as Florida's largest city.

Key West, at the southern tip of the Keys, remained isolated from the rest of the state. The only way in or out of the city was by water. Henry Flagler, aging but full of energy, decided to end the city's isolation by extending the East Coast Railway all the way across the Keys. Some Floridians called the proposed railroad "Flagler's Folly." To reach Key West, the tracks

In this Currier & Ives lithograph, American warships return victorious from a battle in the war with Spain. Much of the Spanish American War was fought in the waters around Cuba—only 90 miles from Miami off the coast of Florida.

would have to cross more than 100 miles of ocean. Nothing like it had ever been attempted before. In a great feat of engineering, Flagler's construction crews succeeded in building the railroad, at a cost of more than $50 million.

Today, the forty-two bridges built to bring the tracks across the water are used by cars traveling Florida's Overseas Highway.

The Land Boom— and Bust

More tourists flocked to Florida in the years after World War I. The age of the automobile was beginning, and the construction of the Dixie Highway and other roads opened Florida to visitors by car. Every winter, thousands of visitors from the Midwestern states drove to Florida to enjoy a week or two in the sun. Old Floridians called these new visitors "tin can tourists" because they camped by the side of the road and brought their own food. Some grumbled that the "tin-canners" didn't contribute much to Florida's economy. "They came to Florida with one suit of underwear and one twenty-dollar bill," said Fuller Warren, a future governor, "and they changed neither."

Tourists with more money to spend made Miami their favorite destination. In the 1920s, the city's population

Together with partner John Collins, Carl Fisher filled in 1,600 acres of swamp to create Miami Beach. This photograph shows the Spanish-style estate that was built for Fisher in 1926. Fisher vowed to "live and die on the island" on which the estate is located, but did neither. The estate was later occupied by William K. Vanderbilt II. Today's Miami skyline appears in the background.

grew from about 30,000 to 110,000. Real estate developers hired William Jennings Bryan, a statesman and also one of the nation's best-known attorneys, to promote the city. Bryan proclaimed Miami to be "the only city in the world where you can tell a lie at breakfast that will come true by evening."

New resort communities sprang up throughout Dade County. Businessman Carl Fisher built Miami Beach on an island made of sand dug from the bottom of Biscayne Bay. Another developer, George Merrick, founded the suburb of Coral Gables. Palm Beach, seventy-five miles north of Miami, became famous as the vacation retreat of millionaires and movie stars.

With so many tourists and so much new construction, land values in South Florida shot up overnight. By the mid-1920s, Florida was in the midst of an amazing real estate boom. Dressed in fancy uniforms, salesmen called "Binder Boys" sold deeds on the streets of Miami while brass bands played. It seemed that everyone who could scrape together the money for a down payment on a piece of property was investing in Florida land. Few of the buyers were interested in living on their land; most just hoped to make a quick profit. Some building lots were bought and sold twenty times in a single day.

The boom died almost as quickly as it had begun. The winter of 1925 was unusually cold, and the summer that followed was terribly hot. Investors and tourists began to doubt the state's reputations as paradise on Earth. Florida was starting to recover when a nationwide depression began in 1929.

Few of Florida's African Americans had shared in the prosperity brought by tourism and agriculture. Many African Americans left Florida to look for jobs in the factories of the Northern states. Most of those who stayed lived a harsh existence on farms in northern and central Florida. In spite of prejudice and hardships, African Americans with roots in Florida accomplished great things in a variety of fields, including educator Mary McLeod Bethune, labor leader A. Philip Randolph, and writers James Weldon Johnson and Zora Neale Hurston.

The great hurricane of 1926 was the final blow to the South Florida land boom of the 1920s. This aerial photograph (top, right) shows the damage to Miami, where extremely high tides added to the destruction caused by heavy winds.

From World War I through the Depression, tens of thousands of Florida's African Americans, including this family shown at right, left the state for better opportunities in the North.

World War II and After

America's entry into World War II in December 1941 helped bring Florida out of the Depression. The state's geography gave it an important role in the nation's war effort.

Because of its year-round warm weather, Florida was a good location for training camps and military bases. The state also had plenty of timber for construction. Before the war ended in September 1945, more than 2 million servicemen and women passed through Florida's training camps. One post—Camp Blanding, near Starke—became the state's fourth-largest city,

with a population of 90,000 soldiers. The military also used many of Florida's famous resort hotels to house trainees. In Miami alone, the army took over 70,000 hotel rooms. Later, the hotels were converted to hospitals for wounded men from the battlefields of North Africa and Europe.

Florida also became home to more than forty military air bases during the war years. Most Marine and Navy pilots trained at the Naval Air Station in Pensacola. Eglin Field was built in the Panhandle to serve the Army Air Forces (later the U.S. Air Force). Throughout the conflict, planes from Florida protected the Panama Canal, the vital passageway connecting the Atlantic and Pacific oceans.

The war often came very close to Florida. German U-boats (submarines) roamed the state's coastal waters, sinking cargo ships and oil tankers—often in full view of people on shore. One night, for example, people enjoying a night out at Jacksonville's amusement park watched in horror as the tanker *Gulfamerica* exploded in flames, victim of a U-boat's torpedo. The U.S. Navy eventually drove the U-boats away, but not before twenty-six merchant ships had been lost.

Florida also received some unexpected and unwelcome visitors in the summer of 1942, when a U-boat secretly landed four German spies and a cargo of explosives on a beach just south of Jacksonville. Burying the explosives, the spies walked to town and registered in local hotels. Luckily, FBI agents had been informed, so the four agents were arrested before they could do any damage.

Thanks to its climate and geography, Florida became a major center for training camps and bases during World War II. In this photo (opposite), crewmen moor a large seaplane at the Banana River Naval Air Station in 1943.

It was not until after World War II that Florida and other Southern states were forced to end their long-standing practice of segregation by race. This 1945 photograph (above) shows a "colored only" store in Belle Glade.

Tourism and Technology

The coming of peace began another boom period in Florida's history, but this one would be much more stable and long-lasting than the wild 1920s. Florida once again played host to millions of tourists in the late 1940s and 1950s—4.5 million people visited Florida in 1950 alone. Between 1949 and 1964, the state government spent millions of dollars to improve the roads, making it easier for tourists to travel into and around Florida. The expansion of Miami International Airport in 1959 did the same for visitors traveling by air.

Florida also attracted a new wave of permanent residents. Between 1940 and 1950, Florida's population grew by 46 percent. Growth in the 1950s was even more spectacular—by the end of the decade, Florida was home to nearly 5 million people.

Some of the newcomers were World War II veterans who had trained or served in Florida and had come to love the mild climate and the scenery. Many others were retired citizens escaping the cold and harsh weather of the Midwestern and Northeastern states. With plenty of inexpensive real estate and low taxes, the state was especially attractive to retirees who had to live on a fixed income. Also, the introduction of affordable air conditioners in the 1950s made Florida's summer heat and humidity less of a problem for residents. By the mid-1980s, one in five Floridians was over sixty-five years of age.

People from the Midwestern states tended to settle along the Gulf Coast, while the Atlantic Coast attracted retirees from the Northeastern states. After about 1960, many Jewish people chose Florida for their retirement homes. By 1990, the Miami area had a Jewish community of more than 600,000 people, the third largest in the country.

In the postwar years, Florida became the headquarters of the nation's new space program. In 1949, the U.S. Air Force bought 12,000 acres of land at Cape Canaveral, in Brevard County on the Atlantic Coast. On July 24, 1950, the first rocket to be launched from the Cape soared into the blue Florida sky.

The coming of the space program touched off a high-tech boom in the towns around Cape Canaveral. Brevard County's population grew by 400 percent as aerospace companies built offices and factories in the area, bringing engineers, technicians, and other workers with them.

Cape Canaveral went into high gear in 1957, when the Soviet Union launched the first artificial satellite, *Sputnik*, starting a space race between

Federal and state highway construction helped bring millions of visitors to Florida in the years after World War II. Shown here is the famous Seven-Mile Bridge, constructed to replace part of the old Overseas Highway that connected mainland Florida to the Keys.

The Kennedy Space Center complex is an important part of the U.S. space program and a major tourist attraction. The vehicle assembly building in this photograph (right) is one of the largest buildings in the world.

the Soviet Union and the United States. Activity on the Cape increased even more after 1961. In that year, the first American astronauts blasted into space from Cape Canaveral, and President John F. Kennedy made it a national goal to land an astronaut on the moon. Two years later, NASA (the National Aeronautics and Space Administration) expanded Cape Canaveral by purchasing an 88,000-acre site on nearby Merritt Island. After President Kennedy's assassination in 1963, the entire complex was renamed the Kennedy Space Center in his honor.

In July 1969, the *Apollo 11* space mission fulfilled President Kennedy's goal by landing two astronauts on the moon. Today, Kennedy Space Center is the launch site for the Space Shuttle, as well as a popular destination for tourists.

Tourism continued to drive Florida's economy as the state entered the 1960s. In the past, Florida's weather and scenery were the major tourist attractions, and most visitors arrived in the winter months. After World War II, however, enterprising developers built attractions to lure tourists to the state year-round.

The best known and most successful of these attractions is Walt Disney World, near Orlando in central Florida. Work on the site began in 1963, and the 28,000-acre theme park opened its gates in 1971. In its first decade, Disney World brought an astonishing $14 billion dollars into the Orlando area's economy. In 1982, a new addition to the Disney complex, EPCOT Center (Experimental Prototype Community of Tomorrow) opened for business.

The success of Disney World led other developers to build attractions throughout Florida, including giant theme parks like Tampa's Busch Gardens and Sea World in Orlando. Hundreds of smaller attractions, from wax museums to roadside alligator farms, also compete for tourist dollars.

Tourists relax at beachside at one of Florida's many resorts (opposite). By the 1980s, 30 million people visited the state each year—and the state gained almost 5,000 new residents every week.

A trainer puts Shamu, a killer whale, through a routine at Sea World in Orlando. Sea World is one of the country's most popular marine life parks, combining entertainment with education, research, and conservation.

Sport fishing, boating, and nature-watching are just some of the activities that bring tourists to Florida. In this photograph (right), visitors enjoy a canoe tour around Big Pine Key.

The New Immigrants

At the same time Cape Canaveral began to hum with activity, trouble was brewing in Cuba. The island had become independent in 1898, but democracy had never taken root. One dictator after another ruled Cuba in the first half of the century. A handful of Cubans grew rich and powerful, while the majority of the people lived in poverty.

In 1959, a young revolutionary named Fidel Castro overthrew the corrupt dictatorship of Fulgencio Batista. Castro promised a fairer, more democratic Cuba. After taking power, however, Castro turned toward communism and announced that Cuba would be an ally of the Soviet Union. Cubans who opposed the new government were killed or imprisoned.

Thousands of Cubans fled their homeland, refusing to stay and live under Castro's rule. Between 1959 and 1979, half a million Cuban refugees came to Florida. About 350,000 of them settled in Miami and other Dade County communities. Refugees from other Latin American and Caribbean nations, especially Haiti, joined the new Cuban Americans in the 1960s and 1970s.

Meanwhile, a stream of newcomers from other parts of the United States continued to flow into Florida. In the 1970s, when many people moved from the "rust belt" of the Northeast and Midwest to the "sun belt" of the South and Southwest, Florida had the highest population growth of any state except California and Nevada.

The arrival of so many new Floridians changed the face of the state forever. Before World War II, Florida was a state of resort hotels, cattle ranches, orange groves, and isolated farms set amid vast swamps and pine forests. By the 1970s, the state had lost much of its old character. In its place was a new state, made up of diverse communities—retirees and refugees, cattle ranchers and high-tech workers—with little in common. One writer described modern Florida as "a collection of cities in search of a state."

The arrival of hundreds of thousands of Cuban refugees gave Miami and other South Florida communities a Latin-American atmosphere. This Cuban-owned business in Miami (opposite) advertises its support of Kennedy's stand during the Cuban missile crisis by showing his picture in its storefront window.

Learning to speak English was the first thing many Cuban refugees needed to do in order to make a living in Florida. This 1963 photo (below) shows an English class for refugees in Miami.

Although an important industry for Florida, phosphate mining was hard on the environment. The mining process made large holes in the earth (left). Through a process called reclamation, however, the land could be made useful when mining was over. All of the land mined after 1975 has been reclaimed, much of it turned into lakes and wetlands.

The Everglades National Park (below), along with the Big Cypress National Preserve, covers the southern tip of Florida. The parks are home to thousands of species of wildlife and are enjoyed by millions of visitors each year.

Florida's rapid growth also put great strain on the state's environment—especially its wetlands, which were hard hit by pollution from new homes and businesses. Floridians began to realize the dangers facing the state's environment in the 1960s, when the state government halted a plan to build a new international airport in the Everglades. In 1974, the state and federal government set aside 570,000 acres of wetlands to establish the Big Cypress National Preserve. South of Big Cypress is Everglades National Park, created in 1947 but greatly expanded by the purchase of 108,000 acres in the early 1990s. The movement to preserve the Everglades was inspired by two influential Floridians: John Pennekamp, editor of the *Miami Herald* newspaper, and historian Marjory Stoneman Douglas who is often called Florida's "resident author." Douglas's best-known work is *The Everglades: River of Grass*.

Despite the wave of newcomers from Cuba and other countries, African Americans remained Florida's single largest minority group, making up approximately 13 percent of the state's population. In the years after World War II, many African Americans moved from rural areas to the state's growing cities, especially Miami. Florida finally ended its long-standing system of racial segregation in the 1960s and 1970s, but many African Americans still endured prejudice, poverty, and other problems.

Racial tensions were running high in Miami as the 1980s began. Some African-American leaders charged that the city and state weren't doing enough to help the black community, while spending millions of dollars to help Cuban immigrants adjust to life in Florida. African Americans faced job competition from Haitians and other newly arrived immigrants. In addition, relations were tense between Miami's African Americans and the city's police force—which was mostly white and Hispanic.

In May 1980, these tensions exploded into violence. In December 1979, Miami police had arrested Arthur McDuffie, an African-American businessman, for a traffic violation. McDuffie died shortly after the arrest. The policemen involved—three white officers and one Hispanic officer—were accused of beating McDuffie to death. On May 17, however, a jury acquitted the officers of all charges of wrongdoing.

When the verdict was announced, three days of rioting swept Miami's mostly African-American Liberty City neighborhood. Eighteen people lost their lives in the violence. Riots hit Miami again in 1982 and 1989. Today, the city is still struggling to heal the ongoing tension between its ethnic communities.

Florida Today

Florida's growth continued in the 1980s and early 1990s. More than 2.5 million people moved to Florida between 1980 and 1990; in 1987, Florida became the nation's fourth-largest state. About 30 million tourists, many from overseas, visited Florida each year in the 1980s.

Another wave of Cuban immigration reached Florida in the beginning of the 1980s. Fidel Castro had kept Cuba's borders closed for years, but in the spring of 1980 he suddenly allowed Cubans to leave the country. Between April and June, boats ferried more than 100,000 people from the Cuban port of Mariel to Florida. The early 1980s also saw a rise in the number of Haitian refugees arriving in the state as political upheavals and violence made that country a dangerous place to live.

These new arrivals didn't receive the same welcome as earlier refugees. For one thing, the Mariel immigrants included many criminals who were being "dumped" into Florida by Castro. Some people questioned whether South Florida could continue to absorb so many people from so many places. Miami's population was now about half Hispanic, and the city's close ties to Latin America and the Caribbean made some English-speaking Floridians anxious. "Will the last American to leave Miami please bring the flag?" read one bumper sticker seen on the city's streets in the 1980s.

The illegal drug trade also became a major problem for the state. In 1982, the federal government estimated that three-quarters of the drugs reaching America's streets came through Florida. With drugs came an increase in crime. Florida's rising crime rate not only made the quality of life worse for many residents; it threatened the state's tourist industry, worth $30 billion dollars a year.

Nature has always been Florida's best friend—and sometimes its worst enemy. In August 1992, the state felt nature's fury when Hurricane Andrew ripped across southern Dade County, leaving 43 people dead and more than 250,000 people homeless.

Despite the problems of the last few years, there are plenty of reasons to be hopeful about Florida's future. Throughout its long history, Florida has always relied on the energy and optimism of its people to overcome great challenges. "Florida," in the words of a state historian, "is a living testament to the American belief that there will always be a tomorrow, the clouds will roll away, and a stunning sun will shine." As the 21st century approaches, Floridians are working hard to make the state's future a bright one.

In the 1980s, thousands of Haitians made the dangerous crossing to Florida in small boats. Many died on the way. This group (left) waits on the beach at Sebastian, Florida, for transportation to Miami, having survived an eight-day boat trip without food or water.

Hurricane Andrew was a great tragedy for Florida. People from all over Florida and the country rushed to help the victims of the storm. In this photo (below), a soldier from Ft. Bragg, North Carolina, helps a family with emergency supplies in Homestead, one of the hardest-hit communities in the state.

Land area:

58,664 square miles, of which 4,511 are inland water. Ranks 22nd in size.

Major rivers:

St. Johns and Apalachicola river systems; the Aucilla; the Choctawhatchee; the Blackwater; the Escambia; the Hillsborough, the Kissimmee; the Ochlockonee; the Perdido; the St. Marys.

Highest point: 345 ft., in Walton County.

Major bodies of water:

Lake Apopka, Big Cypress Swamp; Lake Crescent; the Everglades; Lake George; Lake Kissimmee; Lake Okeechobee. Florida has 1,350 miles of coastline on the Atlantic and Gulf of Mexico.

Climate:

Average January temperature: 67°F
Average July temperature: 83°F

Population: 13,487,621 (1992)
Rank: 4th
    1900: 528,542
    1830: 34,730

Population of major cities (1992):

Jacksonville	635,230
Miami	358,648
Tampa	280,015
St. Petersburg	240,348
Orlando	164,693

Ethnic breakdown by percentage (1990):

White	73.2%
Hispanic	12.2%
African American	13.1%
Asian	1.1%
Native American	3.0%
Other	1.0%

Economy:
    Mining, manufacturing, aerospace, agriculture (cattle, sugarcane, citrus fruits), fishing, shipping, and tourism.

State government:
    Legislature: 40-member senate and a 120-member house. Senators serve for 4 years, representatives for 2.
    Governor: The state's chief executive is elected for a 4-year term.
    Courts: Florida's judicial system includes a state supreme court, appellate courts, circuit and county courts.
State capital: Tallahassee

State Flag

The first state flag was designed in 1868 and adopted, with changes, in 1899. The diagonal red bars symbolize the state's membership in the Confederate States of America during the Civil War. At the center is the state seal.

State Seal

Adopted in 1868, the state seal features the sun's rays, a steamboat, and a Native American scattering flowers.

State Motto

"In God We Trust"—the same motto found on U.S. coins.

State Nickname

Florida is best known as "The Sunshine State" for its sunny weather. Other nicknames include "The Peninsula State" and "The Orange State."

Places

Air Force Museum, Eglin Field

Beal Maltbie Shell Museum, Winter Park

Biscayne National Park, Homestead

Bok Tower Carillon and Gardens, Lake Wales

Bulow Plantation Ruins State Historical Park, Bunnell Beach

Canaveral National Seashore, Cape Canaveral

Castillo de San Marcos National Monument, St. Augustine

Center for the Fine Arts, Miami

Crystal River State Archaeological Site, Crystal River

Cypress Gardens, Winter Haven

Dade Battlefield State Historical Park, Bushnell

De Soto National Memorial, Bradenton

Everglades National Park, Homestead

Florida Caverns State Park, Marianna

Florida State Museum, Gainesville

Fort Caroline National Memorial, Jacksonville

Fort Foster, Zephyrhills

Fort Jefferson National Monument, Dry Tortugas Islands

Gulf Islands National Seashore, Pensacola

Jay Norwood Darling National Wildlife Refuge, Sanibel Island

to See

John Pennekamp Coral Reef State Park, Key Largo

Kennedy Space Center, Cape Canaveral

Koreshan State Historic Site, Estero

Lightner Museum, St. Augustine

Maclay State Ornamental Gardens, Tallahassee

Marjorie Kinnan Rawlings State Historical Site, Gainesville

Merrit Island National Wildlife Refuge, Titusville

Metrozoo, Miami

Naval Aviation Museum, Pensacola

Norton Gallery and School of Art, West Palm Beach

Olustee Battlefield State Historical Site, Olustee

Ringling Museums/Sarasota Jungle Gardens, Sarasota

San Augustin Antiguo, St. Augustine

Sea World, Orlando

Silver Springs, Ocala

Society of the Four Arts, Palm Beach

Stephen Foster State Folk Culture Center, White Springs

Thomas A. Edison Home, Fort Myers

Viscaya Museum of Art, Miami

Walt Disney World/EPCOT Center, Orlando

State Flower

In 1909, the state legislature named the snowy-white orange blossom as Florida's official state flower—a natural choice, because Florida produces more oranges than any other state.

State Bird

The mockingbird won out over the buzzard, the pelican, and other birds in a 1927 contest to choose an official state bird.

State Tree

The sabal palmetto palm, also know as the cabbage palm, became Florida's state tree in 1953.

Florida History

c. 8000 BC Oldest known Native American settlements established

1513 Juan Ponce de Léon claims Florida for Spain

1528 Pánfilo de Narváez explores Florida's Gulf coast

1537 Hernando de Soto lands at Tampa Bay

1564 French Huguenots found Fort Caroline

1565 Spanish forces destroy Fort Caroline and establish St. Augustine, the oldest permanent European settlement in America

1698 The Spanish establish a settlement at Pensacola on the Gulf Coast

c. 1750 Beginning of Creek Indian migration from Georgia to Florida

1763 Spain grants Florida to Britain

1781–83 Spain regains control of Florida following the Revolutionary War

1814 General Andrew Jackson captures Pensacola

1817–18 First war between U.S. forces and Seminole Indians

1819 Spain agrees to cede the Floridas to the U.S. in a treaty that takes effect in 1821

1822 U.S. government unites East and West Florida

1835–42 Second Seminole War; most Seminoles are forced to leave Florida

American

1492 Christopher Columbus reaches America

1607 Jamestown (Virginia) founded by English colonists

1620 *Mayflower* arrives at Plymouth (Massachusetts)

1754–63 French and Indian War

1765 Parliament passes Stamp Act

1775–83 Revolutionary War

1776 Signing of the Declaration of Independence

1788–90 First congressional elections

1791 Bill of Rights added to U.S. Constitution

1803 Louisiana Purchase

1812–14 War of 1812

1820 Missouri Compromise

1836 Battle of the Alamo, Texas

1846–48 Mexican-American War

1849 California Gold Rush

1860 South Carolina secedes from Union

1861–65 Civil War

1862 Lincoln signs Homestead Act

1863 Emancipation Proclamation

1865 President Lincoln assassinated (April 14)

1865–77 Reconstruction in the South

1866 Civil Rights bill passed

1881 President James Garfield shot (July 2)

History

1896 First Ford automobile is made

1898–99 Spanish-American War

1901 President William McKinley is shot (Sept. 6)

1917 U.S. enters World War I

1922 Nineteenth Amendment passed, giving women the vote

1929 U.S. stock market crash; Great Depression begins

1933 Franklin D. Roosevelt becomes president; begins New Deal

1941 Japanese attack Pearl Harbor (Dec. 7); U.S. enters World War II

1945 U.S. drops atomic bomb on Hiroshima and Nagasaki; Japan surrenders, ending World War II

1963 President Kennedy assassinated (November 22)

1964 Civil Rights Act passed

1965–73 Vietnam War

1968 Martin Luther King, Jr., shot in Memphis (April 4)

1974 President Richard Nixon resigns because of Watergate scandal

1979–81 Hostage crisis in Iran: 52 Americans held captive for 444 days

1989 End of U.S.-Soviet cold war

1991 Gulf War

1993 U.S. signs North American Free Trade Agreement with Canada and Mexico

Florida History

1845 Florida becomes 27th state

1855–58 Third and final Seminole War

1860 First railroad linking Atlantic and Gulf coasts is completed

1861 Florida secedes from Union and joins the Confederate States

1864 Battle of Olustee, a Confederate victory, fought in Florida

1865 Florida is placed under military rule following Union victory in the Civil War

1868 New state constitution grants the vote to African Americans

1924–26 A major land boom speeds up Florida's development

1926–28 Hurricanes hit Florida, killing over 2,000 people

1941–45 Military bases built in Florida during World War II

1950 Cape Canaveral chosen as U.S. space center

1959–61 Many refugees leave Cuba for Florida after Castro takes power

1969 Segregation by race ended in Florida's public schools

1980 Race riots claim 18 lives in Miami

1988 State constitutional amendment makes English the official language for state government

1992 Hurricane Andrew leaves 43 dead and 250,000 homeless

Juan Ponce de Léon (1460–1521) This Spanish explorer is the first European known to have landed in Florida. He named the region when he arrived in 1513.

Andrew Jackson (1767–1845) The future president invaded Florida in 1818. When Florida became part of the United States, Jackson served as territorial commissioner and governor until 1822.

John Gorrie (1803–55) A South Carolina-born doctor, Gorrie settled in Florida in 1830. Gorrie invented the first practical mechanical refrigeration system.

Osceola (c. 1803–38) This great Seminole leader refused to leave when the Indians were ordered out of Florida in 1835. Osceola fought a determined guerrilla war until 1837, when he was captured. He died in captivity six months later.

David Levy Yulee (1811–86) Yulee was one of the first U.S. senators from Florida, and the first Jewish senator from any state.

Vincente Martinez Ybor (1818–96) A leading cigar manufacturer, Ybor left Cuba to settle in Florida. He built a flourishing cigar manufacturing complex. Known as Ybor City, the community eventually became part of Tampa.

Henry B. Plant

Henry B. Plant (1819–99) Born in Connecticut, Plant moved to Florida and developed the Gulf Coast by building hotels, railroads, and shipping lines.

Henry Morrison Flagler (1830–1913) Flagler was the driving force behind the East Coast Railway, which opened up Florida's Atlantic Coast to development. He also built a network of resort hotels in the Miami area.

Hamilton Disston (1844–96) Disston drained and improved the swampy land of central Florida, turning it into a major agricultural region.

Ruth Bryan Owen (1855–1954) The daughter of statesman William Jennings Bryan, Ruth Owen became both the first woman elected to the House of Representatives from the lower South in 1929, and the first U.S. woman diplomat in 1933.

Napoleon Broward (1857–1910) Broward was elected governor of Florida in 1900 and worked to overhaul the state's educational system and open the Everglades region to development.

Lue Gim Gong (1858–1925) An Asian-American plant scientist, Gong introduced to Florida a new variety of orange that could survive frost.

James Weldon Johnson (1871–1938) Born in Jacksonville, Johnson was an African-American poet, educator, and scholar. He also served as a U.S. diplomat in Central America.

Carl Fisher (1874–1939)
Fisher moved to Florida in 1915. Using sand from Biscayne Bay, he built the resort community of Miami Beach.

Mary McLeod Bethune (1875–1955) This pioneering African-American educator and civil rights activist founded Bethune-Cookman College in Daytona Beach in 1904.

Joseph W. Stilwell (1883–1946) Stilwell rose to the rank of four-star general in a long military career. In World War II, he commanded U.S. forces in the China-Burma-India theater of the war.

A. Philip Randolph (1889–1979) Born in Crescent City, Randolph founded the Brotherhood of Sleeping

Zora Neale Hurston

Car Porters in 1925, one of the most influential African-American labor organizations.

Marjory Stoneman Douglas (b. 1890) A writer, historian, and conservationist, Douglas is the author of *The Everglades: River of Grass*. This book inspired the movement to preserve the Everglades.

Marjorie Kinnan Rawlings (1896–1953) Rawlings moved to Florida in 1928. She was a writer of books for both adults and young people, and many of her best-known works, including *The Yearling* (1939), are set in the state.

John D. Pennekamp (1898–1978) Editor of the influential *Miami Herald* newspaper, Pennekamp was one of Florida's most important conservationists.

Ernest Hemingway (1899–1961) One of the country's greatest novelists, Hemingway made Key West his headquarters and home from 1928 to 1940.

Zora Neale Hurston (1903–60) A native of Eatonville, Hurston became a leading chronicler of rural

Janet Reno

African-American life and folklore in books such as *Mules and Men*.

Jacqueline Cochran (c. 1912–80) Born into poverty in Pensacola, Cochran became a successful businesswoman before taking up flying in the 1930s. She helped organize the Women Air Force Service Pilots during World War II.

Janet Reno (b. 1938) A native of Miami, Reno served as Florida attorney general from 1978 to 1993. In March of that year, President Clinton made her the first woman to be appointed U.S. attorney general.

Pictures in this volume:

Associated Press/Wide World Photos: 53 (both)

Fisher Development Corporation: 39

Kennedy Space Center/NASA: 45 (bottom)

Library of Congress: 7, 9 (top), 10 (bottom), 11, 12, 13, 15, 17 (bottom), 8, 21, 22, 23, 25 (bottom), 26, 29, 30, 31, 33 (bottom), 35, 36, 38, 41 (both), 48, 57 (bird), 60, 61(left)

Monroe County Tourist Development Council: 45 (top), 46, 47 (bottom)

Museum of Early Southern Decorative Arts: 17

National Archives: 34, 42, 43, 49

NPS/Everglades National Park: 50 (bottom)

New York Public Library: 19

Phosphate Council: 2, 33 (top), 50 (top)

Sea World: 47 (top)

Smithsonian Museum: 9 (bottom)

U.S. Department of Justice: 61 (right)

US Naval Historical Center: 28

About the author:

Charles A. Wills is a writer, editor, and consultant specializing in American history. He has written, edited, or contributed to more than thirty books, including many volumes in The Millbrook Press's *American Albums from the Collections of the Library of Congress* series. Wills lives in Dutchess County, New York.

Suggested reading:

Carpenter, Allen, *Enchantment of America: Florida*, Chicago: The Childrens Press, 1979

Fitcher, George S., *Floridians All*, Gretna, LA: Pelican, 1991

Jahoda, Gloria, *Florida: A Bicentennial History*, New York: Norton, 1976

Morgan, Cheryl K., *The Everglades*, Mahwah, NJ: Troll Associates, 1990

Rawlings, Marjorie K., *Cross Creek*, New York: Macmillan, 1987
—*The Yearling*, (*Scribners Illustrated Classics* Series), New York: Scribners, 1985

Stone Lynn, *America the Beautiful: Florida*, Chicago: The Childrens Press, 1987

For more information contact:

Florida Division of Tourism
Visitor Inquiry Section
126 Van Buren Street
Tallahassee, FL 32301
(904) 487-1462

Historic St. Augustine
Chamber of Commerce
1 Ribera Street
St. Augustine, FL 32084
(904) 825-5033

INDEX

Page numbers in *italics* indicate illustrations